MAGICAL STORIES

Other Walker Treasuries

Animal Stories
Funny Stories
Stories for Five-year-olds
Stories for Six-year-olds

First published 1995 by Walker Books Ltd
87 Vauxhall Walk, London SE11 5HJ

2 4 6 8 10 9 7 5 3 1

Text © 1995 individual authors
Illustrations © 1995 individual illustrators
Cover illustrations © 1995 David Parkins

This book has been typeset in ITC Garamond.

Printed in England

British Library Cataloguing in Publication Data
A catalogue record for this book is
available from the British Library.

ISBN 0-7445-4341-X

MAGICAL STORIES

WALKER BOOKS
AND SUBSIDIARIES
LONDON • BOSTON • SYDNEY

CONTENTS

TILLIE M^cGILLIE'S FANTASTICAL CHAIR

by VIVIAN FRENCH
illustrated by SUE HEAP

Tillie McGillie lived at
the very top of a tall thin
building with eighty-two
steps on the outside.

Tillie McGillie had
10 woolly hats

9 woolly scarves

8 woolly jumpers

7 woolly socks

6 woolly cardigans

5 woolly blankets

4 knitting aunts

3 puffing uncles

2 wobbly legs  *and ...*

one gran who was nearly
a fairy and who came to
tea as a surprise.

"Hello, Gran," said Tillie.

"H'mph," said Gran. "What's all this woolliness?"

"It's my legs," Tillie explained. "The aunts like me to keep warm."

"Pots of tea need keeping warm," said Gran. "Children need fresh air."

Tillie sighed. "Carrying me up and down eighty-two steps makes the uncles puff so."

"H'mph," said Gran. "We'll see about *that*."

The aunts came hurrying in from the kitchen.

"Would you like some tea, Tillie's gran?" said Aunt Agnes.

"Shall we have some toast?" said Aunt Bridie.

"If we had known you were coming we would have made a special cake," said Aunt Clara.

"Are you warm enough, Tillie dear?" said Aunt Doris.

"H'mph," said Gran, very loudly, and she pulled a spotty hankie out of her pocket and waved it.

"Oh! Oh! Oh! Oh!" cried all the aunts as they found themselves circling round and round. Gran waved the hankie again.

"Ooooooooooooooh!" said all the aunts together as they spun out of the front door and away down the eighty-two steps.

9

The three uncles puffed in.

"What's all the noise about?" they asked.

Gran waved her hankie.

"Puff! Puff!" the uncles all shouted together. "Oh – *Puff! Puff! Puff! Puff!"* And they joined hands in a line and went puffing down the stairs after the aunts.

"That's got rid of *them*," said Gran. "Now, child – what shall we do with you?"

"Is that a magic hankie? Are you going to wave it at me?" Tillie asked anxiously.

"Not so easy," said Gran. She stared hard at Tillie's chair. "Is that comfortable?"

"Yes," Tillie said, wondering what was going to happen next.

Gran tapped the little red wheelchair on its back.

"H'mph – we can but try." She shut her eyes very tightly.

"You can hop, you can skip, you can fly through the air –

Tillie McGillie's fantastical chair!"

10

Tillie's chair gave a hop and a skip.

"Hurrah!" Gran gave a little skip herself. "Hold on tightly, Tillie!"

Tillie held on. The little red chair gave a grunt and a cough, and sprang into the air.

"Up … up … up …" it said, in a rusty dusty voice. "Up … up!"

Gran opened the window wide.

"Fresh air," she said firmly as the chair and Tillie flew past her. "Don't forget now!"

Tillie saw Gran waving as the chair soared up into the sky above the building. She wanted to wave back, but she didn't dare let go.

"It's all right, you know," said the dusty little voice of the chair. "I won't drop you. You can wave if you want to."

"Thank you," Tillie said breathlessly, and waved.

"Wheeeee!" said the chair, and flew up and over the roof of Tillie's tall thin block of flats.

Tillie stared. Down below she could see the aunts running round and round after their wool, and the uncles were puffing up and down the eighty-two steps. Sometimes they met each other and then they would stop and bow, and say, "After you!" and, "No, no, dear Henry – after *you*!" but mostly they were too puffed to say anything at all.

"Where to now?" asked the chair. "North, south, east or west?"

"Up," said Tillie. "Up, up, up!"

"If you say so," said the chair, and *Zooooom!* up they went.

Two birds flying past were so surprised that they bumped into each other, and Tillie could hear them squawking angrily behind her.

The chair began to slow down. "Do you want to go *much* higher?" it asked in a breathless voice.

Tillie was about to answer when there was a loud and terrifying roar, and something huge and silvery rushed across the sky just above her head. The little red chair spun round and round in circles and Tillie screamed as she held on as tightly as she could.

"Dear me," said the chair, steadying itself, "that

was a near thing. I feel quite shaken up!"

"Me too," said Tillie. "I don't think I like planes as close as that. Can we go down again?"

"We certainly can." The little red chair began to drop gently down, down, down until they were hovering just above the treetops.

"I can see a pond," Tillie said. "Can we go and look?"

The chair bobbed up and down, and swung Tillie through the air until they were over the pond. A group of children were busy with fishing nets and jamjars, and just as Tillie and the chair arrived a tall girl held up a jar full of small shining fish.

"Whatever are they catching?" Tillie asked.

"Tiddlers," said the chair in a know-it-all voice.

"Oh!" shouted Tillie. *"Oh – look at that little boy! He's just about to fall in – look out! Do look out!"*

Tillie shouted in such a loud voice that all the children jumped and looked wildly around. There was the most enormous splash as not only the little boy but most of the other children fell into the water, and they all began talking and spluttering and waving their arms about.

"Oh dear," Tillie said.

The chair made a quick turn and shot off down the road. Tillie, twisting round to see what was happening, saw the children scramble out of the pond and start to chase after her, dripping trails of weed and water behind them.

"Stop!" they shouted. *"Stop!"*

"Let's hide," said Tillie. "Quick!"

The chair swept up and over a row of shops. A woman with two girls came out of the greengrocer's just as Tillie whizzed past, and she let out a loud shriek and dropped all her shopping. The

two girls fell over the heaps of potatoes and cauliflowers and apples and sat down on the pavement with a flump.

"Oh dear, oh *dear*," said Tillie.

"Wait for us!" shouted the girls. The

chair slid in between two houses, and began to fly upwards.

"Where shall we go now?" Tillie asked. "None of the people down there like us very much – they keep wanting to chase us."

The little chair didn't answer, and Tillie suddenly noticed that instead of flying smoothly they were bumping from side to side and up and down.

"What's the matter?" Tillie patted the chair's arms.

"I think …" the chair wheezed, "that your gran's magic … is wearing … off…"

"Should we stop?" Tillie was anxious.

The chair took a deep breath. "Let's … try … to get home," it said.

"Perhaps I could *wish* us home," Tillie suggested.

"No harm in … trying," said the chair.

Tillie shut her eyes very tightly, and wished as hard as she could.

"I wish – I wish – I wish that Gran
Would send us home as fast as she can!"

Tillie opened her eyes. Nothing happened, but she saw that the chair was flying lower and lower, and giving strange hiccups and jerks as it went.

Tillie sat up straight. "Oh, look! We're nearly there!"

"Ohhhhhh." The chair gave a small sigh, and landed gently on the ground in front of the tall thin building.

"What's the matter? Can't you fly any more?" Tillie patted and stroked the chair. "Dear chair – we had such fun – *oh!*"

Tillie stared. At the far end of the road she could see a group of children – a group of children all waving and running towards her. Behind them was a woman waving a shopping bag.

"It's those children who fell in the pond … and the girls who sat on the potatoes … and their mum! Oh, little chair – what shall we do?"

The little red chair said nothing, but Tillie felt it give the very faintest jump.

"I *know!*" Tillie leant forward, and wriggled and slid out of the chair until she was sitting on the ground.

"There! Now you won't be so heavy – can you fly? Fly up and get Gran – tell her she's got to come and help!"

The chair gave a little skip, and then a hop. Tillie held her breath, and shut her eyes, and wished as hard as she could.

"You can hop, you can skip, you can fly through the air –

Tillie McGillie's fantastical chair!"

There was a whoosh and a swoosh, and Tillie opened her eyes just in time to see the chair speeding up, up, up into the air.

At the same moment the children arrived and all began shouting at once. Then the aunts came hurrying round the corner and started asking Tillie *what on earth she was doing,* and the uncles puffed up as well. They were much too puffed to ask any questions, so they pointed at Tillie and up at the sky

17

over and over again until Tillie felt so battered and muddled by all the noise and arm waving that she hid her head in her hands and wished as hard as she could that they would all go away.

WHEEEEEEEEEEEEEEEEEEEEEE!

There was a sudden and total silence. Tillie peeped between her fingers. Gran was floating down, down, down from the top of the tall thin block of flats. She was sitting in Tillie's fantastical chair, and she was holding her spotty hankie.

"H'mph," she said. "Whatever's going on here?"

"Oh, Gran!" Tillie burst into tears. "I didn't mean to upset all these people! And the aunts and the uncles are all cross as cross can be with me!"

"The best way to help folks forget one thing is to give them another to remember," Gran said, and she waved her spotty hankie.

There was the strangest noise that Tillie had ever heard. It sounded like a mountain pulling up its roots, or a gigantic monster heaving itself awake. The tall thin block of flats swayed, and shook, and trembled – and then rose slowly into the air.

Up it went, higher and higher – and then it began turning and turning – until it was upside down. Slowly, slowly, it began coming down again, and

Tillie and all the others gave a huge sigh as it settled back down on the ground. It looked as if it had always been there, firmly rooted … but now it was upside down.

"There!" said Gran, looking very pleased with herself. "Now the uncles won't have to carry you up and down eighty-two steps. You can wheel yourself in and out just as you please, Tillie McGillie, so there'll be a lot less woolliness and a lot more fresh air. Oh, and don't go worrying yourself about upside-down furniture." Gran waved her hankie a couple more times. "There! It's all as right as ninepence! Go and see!"

Gran helped Tillie back into the little red chair, and Tillie trundled herself into her flat through what had been a front door at the very top of the building … but was now a front door at the bottom. The uncles and aunts crowded after her, still too surprised to say anything.

"It's *lovely!*" said Tillie, looking round.

Gran nodded. "So it is," she said.

The children who had fallen in the pond came rushing in.

"Yippee!" they said. "It's magic! We live right at the top of the flats now, just where we always wanted to, so we can look at the stars at night!" And they all rushed out again to look up at their new, high-up windows.

The woman with the shopping bag and the two girls knocked at the door.

"Good afternoon," she said. "So nice to have new neighbours… We live in the middle flat, you know. Charmed to meet you… Perhaps Tillie would like to play with Susie and Sally sometimes?"

Tillie looked at the girls. She saw that they still had dirty knees from falling over, but they smiled at her.

"Do come," they said together, "we'll call down tomorrow!"

And they hurried out.

Tillie rubbed her nose. "Why aren't they cross any more, Gran?" she asked.

"Like I said," said Gran. "Give folks something new to think of, and they'll forget everything else as like as not." She coughed, and nodded at the aunts and uncles who were skittering about, admiring the new ceilings and floors. "Look at them – they've quite forgotten I've come to tea," she said.

"Well," Tillie said, "they have been rather busy since you came. I'll make the tea for you."

She went towards the kitchen, and then turned back. "Gran," she said, "thank you very much."

"H'mph," said Gran, pulling her spotty hankie out of her pocket.

"Whoops!" said Tillie, and rolled herself quickly into the kitchen … but Gran was only using her hankie to wipe her spectacles.

"H'mph," Gran said to herself quietly. "I'm wiping my spectacles *this* time … but the *next* time I use my spotty hankie … who knows?" And she winked at the little red chair as Tillie came back with the tea things.

THE HAUNTING

by SARAH HAYES
illustrated by HELEN CRAIG

The oldest inhabitant of Crumbling Castle was a little ghost who lived in the bell tower. She had been there every bit as long as the castle itself. She had seen the first cracks appear in the walls and she had heard the first stones go tumbling down the mountainside. But the little ghost did not mind: she liked Crumbling Castle. And when the ogre left, the little ghost stayed on. There was no one to haunt any longer, but a large white owl came to live in the bell tower and kept her company. Life was pleasant but quiet.

Every night the owl would fly off into the darkness, and the little ghost would glide down from the tower. She always took the same route – down the crumbling steps, through the cracked marble hall, across the ballroom floor, along a corridor, and then up the little winding stairs which led to the battlements. It had been years since she had met anyone in the castle and

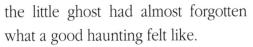

the little ghost had almost forgotten what a good haunting felt like.

When the wizard arrived at the castle, with a line of bags and boxes bumping along behind him, the little ghost was overjoyed.

"At last," she cried, "someone new to haunt!"

"Who's new?" asked the owl, who was sitting on the great bell in the tower.

"The new owner of the castle, of course," said the ghost, "and that thing on his shoulder. I'm going to haunt them."

"You?" asked the owl.

"Of course me," said the little ghost. "There isn't anyone else, is there?"

"True," answered the owl. Then she swivelled her head round and closed her big yellow eyes. She never said much.

"I know I'm going to terrify them," said the little ghost.

"You do, do you?" hooted the owl. She opened both eyes very wide and stared at the little ghost. Then she spread her wings and took off. The great bell hummed faintly.

Some weeks later the little ghost was not so sure of herself. She had practised wailing and shrieking. She had opened and closed creaking doors. She had hidden in cupboards and jumped out. She had glided along the battlements while the wizard Zebulum was stargazing. She had done all the right things, but the wizard just did not seem to notice her.

"He's too busy arguing with that bird of his," she told the owl, "and when he does see me, he looks straight through me."

The owl blinked and said nothing.

"What am I going to do?" wailed the ghost.

"Do to who?" hooted the owl. Sometimes she could be very annoying.

The little ghost lost her temper. "The wizard of course. That stupid, deaf, absent-minded, short-sighted, unobservant old man in the bent hat!"

At that moment Jason flew up. "You must be talking about my master," he said. He landed on the bell with a thump.

The owl ruffled her feathers disdainfully. She looked at Jason through half-closed eyes. "Who are you?" she asked.

Jason drew himself up. "I am the raven Jason," he said solemnly, "familiar and aid to the wizard Zebulum."

"Raven indeed!" said the little ghost who had been watching the two birds with interest. "You're nothing but a common crow!"

Jason's spiky feathers stood on end. His eyes started out of his head and he stared about him. Then he hopped in a circle, looking all round. The owl closed her eyes: crows were not of interest to her.

"If you want to know, I *was* talking about your master," said the little ghost.

Jason jumped at the sound of her voice.

He peered at the owl, who seemed to be fast asleep. He closed his own eyes. "Who's that talking?" he asked in a very small voice.

"The ghost of Crumbling Castle," replied the ghost. Then she did a little wail.

"Caw, caw," came Jason's raucous laugh. "If you're a ghost, where are you?"

The little ghost glided over to the bell and hovered next to Jason. "I'm here," she cooed.

Jason put out a wing. He felt something cold and damp. "I can feel you," he said, "but I can't see you. You must be one of those invisible ghosts."

"Not at all," said the ghost indignantly. "I'm the texture of clouds with trails of mist." The little ghost did not know it, but over the years she had begun to fade.

Jason peered hard. "Can't see a thing!" he said. Then a cloud passed over the sun, and Jason caught the faint shadow of a small but definitely ghostly shape. Things like cobwebs trailed off the end of her skirts, and two grey smudges peered at him from the top. "You *are* a ghost!" he said, but the sun came out of the clouds, and all that was left was a vague outline which disappeared almost immediately. "You've gone again," he announced.

The little ghost was horrified. "No one in my family has ever become invisible before!" She glided over to the owl. "Why didn't you tell me?" she wailed. The owl woke up and blinked rapidly.

Jason looked sideways at the owl's yellow eyes. He did not want to stare. "Owls can't see much by day," he whispered to the ghost, "and I expect you show up a bit at night."

"I hope so," said the little ghost gloomily. "No wonder the wizard looks straight through me."

Jason put his head under his wing for a minute. That was his thinking position.

"What makes ghosts fade?" he asked at last.

The ghost reeled off the

answer: "A ghost will fade in the wrong place, at the wrong time, or in the wrong mood."

Jason thought about that. A ruined castle was certainly the right place for a ghost.

"I always wait till midnight," said the ghost. "We get these shivery feelings which tell us it's the right time."

"So you've got the right place and the right time," said Jason. "But what about the right mood? What is the right mood for a ghost?"

The little ghost spoke as if repeating a lesson. "In order to frighten, a ghost must know fear. A frightened ghost is a fearsome ghost."

Jason hopped up and down on the great bell, which gave a hollow ring. He thought he knew the answer. "What are you afraid of?" he asked.

"Oh, lots of things," the ghost replied. "When I came to the castle years ago, I was scared of everything – the booming and clunking, and the rats and the toads and the dripping; even my friend the owl."

"And now?" asked Jason sternly. "What are you afraid of now?"

The ghost thought hard. Then she spoke in a thin voice. "I see what you mean. I don't think I'm afraid of anything."

"Nothing at all?" asked Jason. "Not even ravens?"

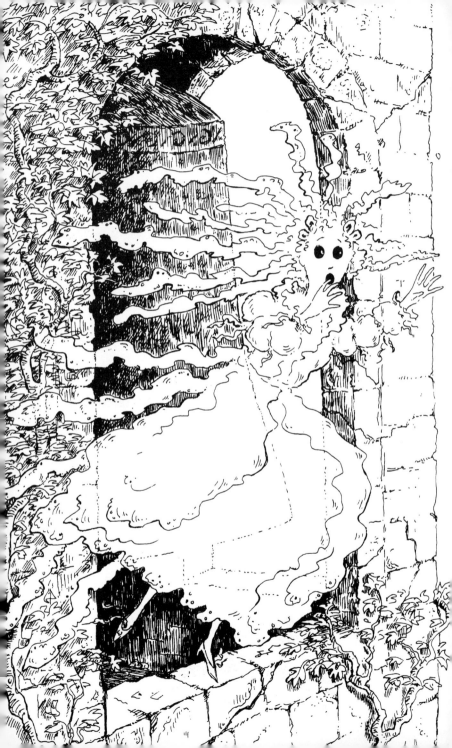

"Ravens are just large crows!" scoffed the ghost.
Jason fluffed out his feathers.

"Not skeletons?" he asked.

"What, afraid of old janglebones – not me!" said the
ghost, and she gave a little hiccupping wail that Jason
thought must be ghostly laughter.

"Not vampire bats or bottomless pits or creaking
coffins or giant spiders?" asked Jason.

"Not a bit!" said the ghost firmly.

"Oh dear," said Jason, "this is going to be harder
than I thought."

The owl woke up and added, "Too true."

"You're not a lot of help," snapped Jason. Then he
gathered himself together for flight. "I'm going to have
a look in my master's books." He spread his wings
and took off. "Back to the beetles in the basement," he
called. Then he stopped in mid-flight.

The ghost had suddenly become quite white and
fluffy, and long streamers trailed out behind her.
"What did you say?" she shrieked.

Jason swooped down to the tower again. "I said back to the beetles in the basement!"

The ghost grew very large and thick and cloudy. Her eyes were black tunnels. Jason wasn't bothered by ghosts, but even he felt a sudden shudder. The ghost was wailing: "Not beetles," she moaned. "Not black beetles!"

So that was it, thought Jason. Everyone was afraid of something, and the little ghost was terrified of black beetles. Now Jason knew exactly what to do.

That afternoon Jason worked very hard in the wizard's basement. He told Zeb that the cracks in the floor needed filling in – two dragon's teeth had already been lost down there. The wizard mixed a special elastic filling material which would stretch if the cracks got any wider, and Jason spent several hours pushing in the filler with his beak. He couldn't talk much, so the wizard was able to work in peace. Zeb was delighted. Once or twice he wondered what Jason was planning, but he was too busy perfecting finger-lightning to pay much attention.

Jason filled in all but one of the cracks in the floor. Then he waited. As the sun went down, a black beetle appeared out of the crack. Jason rapped the floor with his beak. "I want the biggest, blackest beetle you've got," he said. "Pass it down the line."

More beetles came out of the crack and began whispering to one another. Soon the floor was thick with beetles, murmuring and buzzing and clicking away to each other. They were all ordinary small beetles, Jason noticed with disappointment. Then the crowd of beetles began to edge away from the crack. The clicking grew intense. Jason watched eagerly as a pair of huge feelers appeared. Then a perfectly enormous beetle emerged from the crack. It was ten times as big as the others.

Jason smoothed down his feathers. "Harken to the raven," he began. The beetles clicked and buzzed loudly. Jason started again. "Listen to the crow, I mean," he said hastily. The beetles were quiet. "If you do not do as I ask, I shall seal the last crack in the floor and close your home for ever."

The giant beetle raised a leg, which Jason thought was a good sign. "I shall need your help once a year," he continued, "but I mean you and your people no harm." The beetle waved its leg. Jason bent right down. He could see himself reflected hundreds of times in the huge beetle's eye. He tweaked his feathers into place. Then he outlined his plan.

A minute before midnight the little ghost felt her usual shivering feeling. "Time to go to work," she said. The moon was shining brightly, and the ghost was no more than a faint haze against the darkest part of the sky. She floated down from the bell tower, wailing gently. Halfway down, a lump of stone dislodged itself from the wall and went crashing down the steps. It made a tremendous noise in the silence, but the little ghost did not seem to hear it. She lingered in the marble hall and shrieked as horribly as she could. Anyone listening would have thought it was the wind whistling, for over the years the little ghost's voice had grown very faint.

Through the marble hall she went, across the ballroom where a large spider sat in a pool of moonlight, and into the long corridor. The wizard was nowhere about, but the little ghost opened and closed a few doors anyway because that was what she did every night. When she reached the battlements, she paused. The wizard was in his favourite position, leaning against the wall looking up at the sky. On fine nights he often stood there for an hour or more gazing at the stars. Tonight, however, he threw out his hands and nodded happily as several small sparks came from his fingertips.

There were others besides the little ghost who were watching the wizard practise finger-lightning. Up in the tower sat two birds, perched at a little distance from each other on the great bell. Jason was trying not to laugh, and the owl, who had been out hunting, was sitting hunched up with closed eyes, paying no attention to what was going on below.

Somewhere, a slate crashed to the ground. The castle shook slightly and the little ghost began to glide towards the wizard. Jason peered down from the tower. The owl opened her eyes a slit. The shadowy outline of the ghost reached the wizard. Zeb shivered and pulled his cloak round his shoulders.

Then the little ghost saw the beetle.

Nestling in the bent tip of the wizard's hat, waving his feelers slightly, sat the largest, blackest, most terrifying beetle the ghost had ever seen. She screamed. She screamed a scream which tore across the sky and froze the water in the streams for miles around. The wizard fell backwards. Rigid with terror, Jason watched from his perch on the bell. He saw the ghost grow thick and white. Then he saw the huge beetle open its wings and fly up over the battlements. The scream came again and again. The crow and the owl toppled off their perches, and the great bell swung. For the first time in a hundred years, the rusty clapper clanged. The bell rang hollowly. Jason and the owl began to plummet to the ground.

The ghost screamed again and again. The toads in the basement tried to hide under each other. The spider lay on her back in the pool of moonlight on the ballroom floor. The rats and mice and bats stopped squeaking. Only the giant beetle moved. It flew calmly on, down towards the basement. Its job was done.

As for the ghost, she was now a fearsome figure, and her white trails stretched the whole length of the battlements. The wizard Zebulum opened his eyes. At first he thought a fog had come down over the castle. Then he saw two great black holes glaring at him, and the swirling trails of mist. "A phantom," he whispered, and fainted.

The ghost looked anxiously at the wizard's fallen hat. The beetle had gone. But the thought of it was enough to make her scream again and grow cloudy. Then she pulled herself together.

She swooped round and round, admiring the way her trails rippled over the walls. As her fear left her, she began to regain her normal size, but she was no longer just a hazy outline. Thick and white as cotton wool, she danced up the tower steps.

The ghost was filled with pride. No one had ever called her a phantom before. And no one had rung the great bell in living memory – how had she managed that? Altogether it had been a haunting to remember. She hoped someone had seen her. Perhaps the owl had been watching. The ghost floated up to the bell, but her friend was not there.

The owl was lying on the ground at the foot of the castle. Terrified by the ghost and deafened by the noise of the bell, the two birds had fallen senseless from the tower. A few metres from the ground Jason realized what was happening. He spread his wings just in time, and made a bumpy landing. The owl was not so lucky. She had fallen all the way. Jason stumbled over to her. The owl lay quite still. Then the yellow eyes fluttered and opened. "Good for you," she hooted faintly.

"Yes, ravens certainly know a thing or two," said Jason. The owl opened her eyes very wide and stared hard at Jason. "And crows know even more," he added. Then he said quickly, "Let's fly back to the tower."

The owl struggled to her feet. "Too bruised," she said.

"We'll just have to walk," said Jason.

The wizard was recovering in his favourite chair when the two birds limped past him. He couldn't be sure, but he thought he heard them laughing.

UNDER THE MOON

by VIVIAN FRENCH
illustrated by CHRIS FISHER

Once upon a time there was a little old woman and a little old man who lived together in a little old house. They would have been very happy but for one thing: the little old woman just could not sit still. Never, ever did she sit down and share a cup of cocoa with the little old man. Dust, dust, dust, polish, polish, polish, shine, shine, shine – all day long she was busy.

The little old man began to sigh, and to grow lonely. While their ten tall children were growing up in their neat little house he didn't have time to notice how the little old woman never stopped working. Now, however, he liked to sit by the fire and dream, and he thought it would be a friendly thing if the little old woman sat beside him.

"You could knit a little knitting," said the little old man, "or sew a little seam?"

But the little old woman said, "No, no, no! I must dust and sweep and clean."

The little old man sighed a long sad sigh and went and put the kettle on. He sat down beside the fire with Nibbler the dog and Plum the cat, and Nibbler curled up at his feet and Plum curled up on his lap, but still the little old man felt lonely.

The little old woman went on sweeping the yard with her broom, even though the stars were beginning to twinkle in the sky.

One day there was a knocking on the door.

"Who's there?" asked the little old woman, running to open the door with her duster in one hand and her mop in the other.

"It's me," said young Sally from the cottage down the road. "My mum says you're the bestest cleaner in all the village, and we've just got two new babies as like as two peas, and all the children running here and there with smuts on their noses and dirt on their toeses, and our mum was a wondering...?"

The little old woman didn't wait another moment. She picked up her broom as she ran through the door, and she fairly flew down the road to Sally's cottage. All day she polished and swept and scrubbed and by the time the stars were twinkling, the cottage down the road was as shiny as a new pin; as fresh as a daisy; as polished as a one-minute chestnut fallen from the tree.

"Well, well, well," said the little old man as she hurried through the door. "There's a good day's work you've done. Would you like a little cocoa?"

The little old woman actually sat down.

"Thank you kindly, my dear," she said. "Just a sip or two – and then I must polish our own little house." And she sat quietly beside the little old man for five minutes.

"This is fine and dandy," said the little old man, smiling. Nibbler laid his head on the little old woman's feet, and Plum purred happily.

"Just as it should be of a gentle summer evening," said the little old man.

"No, no, no!" said the little old woman. She drank the last drop of her cocoa and jumped to her feet. "It was very nice, but I must hurry, hurry, hurry." And she seized the duster and hurried off to the dresser full of china to polish and shine. The little old man sighed, but it was a medium-sized sigh.

"Five minutes is five minutes more than nothing," he said. Nibbler nodded his head.

The next day brought another knocking on the door.

"Who's there?" said the little old woman, running to the door with her dustpan in one hand and a broom in the other.

"It is I," said the parson from the church across the hill. "I have heard that you are the most wonderful cleaner in the county, and my church is full of mice and moths and mildew."

The little old woman didn't wait another moment. She picked up her soap and a bucket as she ran through the door, and she hurried and scurried to the church across the hill. She swept and she dusted and she rubbed, and by the end the church was glowing as if a hundred candles had been lit inside.

"Well, well, well," said the little old man as she walked through the door. "There's another good day's work done. Could you fancy a cup of cocoa?"

"Thank you kindly," said the little old woman, and she sat down on the bench by the fire with a flop. "Just a small cup, and then I must scrub our own back yard." But she sat quietly with the little old man and with Nibbler the dog and Plum the cat for ten long minutes. Then, up she hopped and away she went with the broom in the yard.

The little old man sighed a very little sigh.

"What do you think, Nibbler? Isn't ten minutes ten whole minutes more than nothing?"

Nibbler nodded, and Plum purred.

The next day no one came to the house. The little old woman cleaned and rubbed and scrubbed her little house inside and out, and when the stars began to twinkle in the bluebell sky she was still swishing her soapsuds in the tub. Then there came a knock at the door – such a timid, quiet little knock you could hardly hear it. The little old woman hurried to see who it was, her hands wet and dripping.

"Who's there?" she asked.

Standing on the doorstep was a strange grey shadow of a man. His hair was long and silver, and his clothes were all a tremble about him.

"I hear," he whispered in a voice as soft as a bird's breath, "that you are the very best cleaner in all the ups and downs of the Earth?"

The little old woman nodded briskly. She shook

the water from her hands, and the drops flew through the air.

"How can I help you?" she asked.

"It's the cobwebs," said the silvery grey person. "I don't know what to do about them."

The little old woman ran back into the house and picked up her broom and a basket of dusters.

"Just tell me where they are," she said fiercely. "I've never met a cobweb yet that didn't whisk away when I got busy."

The silvery grey person waved his arms in the air, and silver dust scattered about him.

"Up there," he whispered, "seventeen times as high as the moon."

The little old woman looked up into the night sky. Sure enough, there, high above the moon, were long trails of cobweb lying across the sky. She hurried inside, and shook the little old man from his doze in front of the rosy crackling fire.

"Come along, my dear," she said, "I need your help."

Nibbler and Plum ran out with the little old man, but when Nibbler saw the stranger he began to whine. He lowered his head, and crawled back into the house with his tail tucked under him. Plum was not afraid. She greeted the grey person as an old friend, purring and rubbing in and out of his legs.

"Whatever is it?" asked the little old man.

"We need your help," said the little old woman. She shook the dusters out of the basket, and settled herself and her broom inside.

"Now, my dear, toss me up, just as high as ever you can."

The little old man picked up the basket. He shut his eyes and counted to three. Then, with a heave and a pitch and a toss, he threw the little old woman up and up and up into the air. Up she flew, higher and higher, until the little old man could only see her as a tiny speck against the light of the moon.

The silvery grey stranger bowed a long and quivery bow.

"I do thank you," he said in his soft thread of a voice, and he shook himself all over. Silvery sparkles flew in the air and settled on the little old man and on the ground around him; it made him sneeze – once, twice, three times.

When he had stopped sneezing the stranger was gone – flown back to his home in the moon. Looking up, the old man could see his pale face smiling down.

* * *

The little old woman came back with the sunlight in the early morning. She slept a little in her rocking chair, and then bustled about the house. It seemed to the little old man that she was not as quick as usual. Perhaps she was tired?

When evening came the little old man put on the kettle, and sat down in front of the fire. Nibbler and Plum sat down with him, and so did the little old woman.

"That's a fine night's work," said the little old man, looking up into the clear and starlit sky. "Not a trace of a cobweb can I see."

The little old woman sniffed. "Indeed, I should hope not, my dear," she said. "When has a cobweb ever been too much for me and my broom? I shall be up again next full moon, just to make sure."

"Would you like a little cup of cocoa?" the little old man asked.

"Indeed I would, my dear," said the little old woman. "And, if it's all the same to you, I'll just sit quietly here this evening. It's tiring work, sweeping all those cobwebs away."

The little old man and the little old woman sat happily together. Nibbler slept curled up at their feet, and Plum settled himself on the little old woman's lap.

It was the same the next night and every night until the full moon rose, and then once more the little old woman seated herself in her basket and the little old man tossed her up into the sky.

"Wheeeee!" she called, as she flew up and up and up. "Can you see me, my dear?"

"I can see you," the little old man said, smiling.

"Will you come with me next time the moon is full?" asked the little old woman.

"No, not I," said the little old man, and he went into the house as the little old woman flew up and away out of sight.

I'll sit by myself tonight, he thought as he put wood on the fire and the kettle on to boil, but she'll be here tomorrow and every night before the next full moon.

Up in the sky the little old woman was sweeping away the cobwebs. Down below the little old man was rocking in his chair, while the kettle bubbled happily on the hearth. The man in the moon smiled at them both, and the silver moon sparkles glistened and shone in the little old man's hair. Nibbler and Plum slept peacefully, and there was not so much as the smallest of sighs in the little old house under the moon.

BEWARE THE KILLER COAT

by SUSAN GATES
illustrated by JOSIP LIZATOVIĆ

I knew at once that the coat didn't like me. It scowled at me from a rail in the second-hand shop.

"But I want a new coat!" I told my mum. "Not a second-hand coat!"

"This is a lovely coat," she said. "It's a bargain! It's good as new!"

I scowled at the coat. The coat scowled back at me with its rows of little metal teeth.

It was a big, red, shiny coat, all puffed up like a poison toad. The flaps on the front were wicked green eyes glinting at me. The zips were iron teeth snarling at me.

Yes, I hated that coat as soon as I saw it.

55

"Aren't you lucky to find a coat like this," said Mum. "I can't think why nobody else has bought it!"

But I knew why. It was waiting. Waiting especially for me. And I didn't feel lucky at all!

"Try it on, Andrew. Red is nice and cheerful."

"It's too big. I'm taking it off. I'm taking it off now, Mum!"

But it wouldn't come off. The coat wouldn't let me go!

"The zip's stuck, Mum. I'm trapped!"

"Stop screaming, Andrew. I'll just pull it off over your head."

Mum tugged and tugged. But the coat held on. It swallowed my head! I was trapped in the dark. The coat clung round my face like an octopus.

I yelled in panic. But the coat crammed my mouth with red shiny stuff so nobody could hear.

Then *pop!* I suddenly saw daylight. Free at last! Mum had saved me.

"Don't buy it, Mum," I begged her. "It's a Killer Coat! It wants to hurt me!"

"Andrew, you do say the weirdest things! You're letting your imagination run away with you again!"

And Mum made me carry the coat all the way home.

After that, the coat behaved itself for a bit. Then it started eating the notes I brought home from school. Very important notes. It did it just to get me into trouble!

"Andrew!" said my mum. "Why didn't you bring home that note about Parents' Evening?"

"But I put it into my coat pocket. Right after the teacher gave it to me. It's in here somewhere."

I put my hand cautiously through the metal teeth and into the black hole beyond. My hand went down and down, right up to my elbow! There were black tunnels inside the coat, tunnels from every pocket. There was a maze of dark tunnels inside that coat! Quickly I snatched my hand back.

"That pocket goes on for ever."

"Don't be silly," said Mum. "There's a hole in it, that's all."

And then my new gloves disappeared. I didn't lose them. I put them in my pocket. I know I did. But the coat ate them. They are probably still in there, in the coat, chewed up inside its huge stomach.

And the coat carried on getting bigger and bigger. It swelled up, bulging like a muscle man – getting stronger and fiercer, so that it could get me when nobody was looking.

"It's eaten my new gloves," I told Mum. "I didn't lose them. Honest!"

"Sometimes, Andrew, I wonder what's going on inside that head of yours," Mum said. "They've probably fallen into the lining. Put your hand in and see."

No fear! I wasn't going to put my hand in there, through those metal teeth and deep, deep down inside the coat. What if it grabbed me and chewed my fingers? What if it gnawed them down to the bone? What if, when it had finished, it gave a great belch and let my hand go, and all that was left was a skeleton claw, waggling on the end of my arm?

In the middle of the night something woke me up. What was that noise? My toes curled up in fright. Then I saw the Killer Coat hanging on my bedroom door. It glowed red in the darkness. It was humpy, like a humped-back troll. It was red and bulgy, like an Alien Thing from outer space. I saw a mean, green eye. It stretched out a long red arm.

Then, *flop!* it leapt down from the peg and a bright red tongue, long as a chameleon's, uncurled. It slithered across the floor!

"Help!" I cried. "The coat is coming to get me! The coat is coming to get me!"

"Andrew! What's the matter?"

It was Mum. She switched on the light. And the Killer Coat just lay there, good as gold, pretending that it wasn't creeping up on me.

She picked up the coat. The red tongue was dangling down its back. And the coat was grinning at me with its little silver teeth as if to say, "Next time, Andrew. Next time. When we're quite alone."

"It's all right, Andrew, you've had a bad dream," said Mum. "Just look! Your coat's an even better winter coat than I thought! It's got a nice red hood that you can zip away."

And she rolled up the red tongue and put it behind the shiny teeth.

Then she hung it back behind my bedroom door.

The next morning, the coat did its most evil thing yet. It ate my pet rat.

When I had friendly coats, Ratty went everywhere in my pockets.

But I didn't dare put him inside the Killer Coat.

That morning, though, he looked so miserable locked inside his cage that I decided to take him to school.

At first the coat behaved itself. We went along the road to school with Ratty peeping out of my pocket watching the world go by – just as he'd done in my old, friendly coat.

When I got into the playground, I reached into my

pocket to show Ratty to my friends. But he wasn't
there.

"Ratty! Ratty!" I cried. I could feel him, running
about inside my coat. My friends could see him,
trapped beneath the shiny red material.

"He's there!"

"No, he's there!"

"He's wriggling round your back!"

"He's running up your arm!"

My coat was moving, wobbling like a giant
strawberry jelly. There were bulges plopping out all
over it!

It was Ratty, in a panic, lost inside those deep dark tunnels and trying to get out.

But I knew he would never get out. The Killer Coat would eat him.

But I knew that Ratty hadn't run away. I knew that he was somewhere deep inside the coat with my new gloves and those very important notes from school – the ones Mum said that I'd lost. Ratty had been gobbled up, like all those other things.

After that, the coat grew very big indeed. It swelled up, as if it were proud of itself. It puffed up like a shiny red zeppelin. Its teeth grinned like sharks' teeth. And its mean, green eyes glowed like traffic lights. It was stronger and fiercer than ever. And I knew that it wouldn't be long now. It was only waiting – waiting until we were quite alone.

That night I had a dream about the Killer Coat. I dreamed I tamed it like a lion-tamer. It growled and roared and showed its teeth.

But I cracked my lion-tamer's whip and made it afraid of me. It whimpered with fear! I cracked my whip and made it do tricks. I made it jump through burning hoops.

And all the people at the circus cheered and cheered.

But it wasn't true – it was only a dream. Because when I woke up next morning the coat was hanging on the peg behind my bedroom door. And it wasn't tame at all. It had grown even bigger, even fiercer during the night. It seemed to fill the room.

I looked round my bedroom floor. Why was it so

tidy? Where were all my piles of books, my heaps of Lego? The coat had eaten them, so that it would grow stronger and stronger and get me when nobody was there.

I was really angry. I jumped on the coat and dragged it off the peg. We had a terrific fight. I punched and kicked, but the coat was winning!

It pulled my hair with its metal teeth.

We rolled over and over, all round the room. It wrapped me up in its long slithery arms so I looked like an Egyptian mummy.

Help! Help! Get me out of here!

"Take that! Take that, you horrible coat!" I shouted.

I thumped it, but it wouldn't let me go. It was squeezing me, tighter and tighter!

The bedroom door opened.

"Andrew! What on earth are you doing? Leave that coat alone!"

Phew! Saved again. It was Mum – just in time.

"I tidied this room up last night," my mum was shouting, "while you were asleep. Now look at the mess in here!"

"It wasn't me," I tried to say. "It was the coat. The coat started it!"

But Mum wasn't listening. "Just look at the state of your coat now."

The coat was lying there, behaving itself, pretending to be good. It let my mother pick it up.

It even smiled at her.

My mum carried the coat downstairs and it lay quite still in her arms, like a baby fast asleep.

She said, "This coat's dirty now. I'll have to put it in the washing machine. And when it's clean again, I want you to look after it. Then it'll last the whole winter!"

By then the coat would have got me, for certain. My mum would come to wake me up for school one morning and she'd push my door. But it wouldn't open. For behind it would be the Great Man-eating Killer Coat, swelling up, filling the whole room, like a big, red, roaring monster! There would be no sign of me. Then the coat would gobble up my mum and grow and grow and burst right through the roof of our house!

It would chase after people, scooping them up with its big red tongue the size of a football field. And when it had eaten all the people on our street, it would move to another street. Then to another town. It would stomp across the countryside and its roars would shake the sky! It would swim the oceans, munching whales, nibbling sharks for snacks.

Nothing could stop it. It would swell and swell until it filled the planet, filled the universe...

Andrew! Are you daydreaming again? Come and practise your recorder!

Good as gold, the Killer Coat let Mum put it into the washing machine. The water rushed into the machine and the Killer Coat began to squirm and thrash about.

For a moment I was really scared. I almost ran after my mum shouting, "Wait for me!"

I thought, What if it smashes through the glass to get at me! What if it drags me into the machine and I get washed and rinsed and spun dry! What if…

But then the bubbles frothed and I couldn't see the coat any more.

A mean, green eye whipped past behind the glass.

Metal teeth scowled at me and vanished in the foam. The Killer Coat spun faster, faster. Now I couldn't see its eyes or teeth at all.

It was just a red blur.

And then a strange thing happened. The white foamy bubbles began turning red.

What's going on? I thought, alarmed.

The red whirlpool in the machine swirled and swirled and swirled around … then it rushed away!

I waited. Nothing happened. I crawled to the machine, pressed my nose against the glass and peered inside.

I could hardly believe it. The Killer Coat wasn't red any more. It was pink. Pale pink! Its eyes were not a fierce and glowing green, but pink as well, like the eyes of white rabbits. And the coat was small now. Not swollen up with shiny red muscles, but shrivelled, like a pink balloon gone pop.

My mum came back into the kitchen.

"What's happened to your coat?" she said.

"Don't ask me," I said. "I only just noticed."

I tried to look serious. But I was smiling like mad behind my hand. For when my mum pulled out the Killer Coat, all pink and wrinkly, it didn't look dangerous at all. And the best thing was, it wouldn't fit me any more!

"It's shrunk. What a pity!" Mum said. "And the colour's all run."

"Throw it in the dustbin," I begged. "It's no use now."

I really thought that she was going to do it. But, at the very last moment, as she was opening the back door, something made her change her mind.

"I don't think I will throw it away," she said. "Someone might want it. I'll give it to a jumble sale."

I thought I saw the Killer Coat grin at me with its wicked little teeth.

So watch out, if you're going to a jumble sale. Watch out for the Killer Coat. It doesn't look dangerous.

It's pink now, with two pink flaps on the front. But don't be taken in by its disguise. It's still the same old Killer Coat. Don't be fooled if it just lies there, looking good as gold.

It's just pretending.

It looks small now. But it'll soon start growing. School notes (very important ones) are its favourite snack, and new gloves and pet rats. And *you*, if you're not very, very careful.

Beware the Killer Coat!

THE ANGEL WHO LOST HIS CLOUD

by MARTIN WADDELL
illustrated by PATRICK BENSON

Fred wanted to be an Angel.

Being an Angel doesn't just *happen*. You have to work at it. You have to be very good for a long time and pass all the Angel Exams, and then you get made into one.

Fred was good, for ages and ages and ages, even on Saturdays. He practised hard on the harp, and he was kind and generous and unselfish and he learned to sing cheerfully, although not always in tune.

One day Wortsley, the Chief Inspector of Angels, called Fred up to his cloud, which was a very special one with a silver lining.

"Congratulations, Fred!" Wortsley said. "You have passed your Angel Exams!"

"Yippee!" cried Fred, throwing his harp up in the air. It went up a long way and hit a passing Saint on the ear.

"Ouch!" said the Saint. "Who threw that harp?"

"Oh, *gosh*!" said Fred. "I'm terribly sorry. It was me!"

"I forgive you," said the Saint. Saints are like that.

"Not a good start, Fred," said Wortsley, with a frown.

"I promise it won't happen again," said Fred.

"See that it doesn't," said Wortsley. "As I was saying, Fred, you have done well in your examinations, apart from your singing, which is terrible!"

"I'm sorry about my singing," said Fred. "I promise I will practise."

"You'll have to," said Wortsley. "For now, you must stand at the back of the Heavenly Choir and open your mouth, but don't sing. Do you understand?"

"Understood," said Fred.

"No singing then," said Wortsley. "No flying until you've passed your Wings Test, and no harp throwing."

"Certainly no harp throwing," said Fred.

"Before you can become a fully-fledged Angel, Fred, you need some practical experience. I'm going to let you out on trial, and see how you get on when you have problems to cope with."

"Oh," said Fred, looking very serious.

"It won't be easy," said Wortsley.

"I know that, Wortsley," said Fred.

"I'm going to start you off tomorrow," said Wortsley. "The question is, what sort of Angel do you want to be?"

"What sorts of Angels are there?" said Fred, who had been so busy wanting to become an Angel of any sort that he hadn't stopped to think about the details.

"All sorts!" said Wortsley. "Some Angels spend all day Harp Playing and some Angels are on the Keep Heaven Tidy Campaign and some Angels look after Lost Causes and some Angels go around being Generally Helpful, but I had something special in mind for you to begin with."

"That's very kind of you, Wortsley," said Fred.

"Angels are very kind," said Wortsley. "You ought to know that."

"Yes, Wortsley," said Fred.

"I thought we might start you off with Urgent Prayers," said Wortsley.

"Oh!" said Fred. "*Big* Ones?"

"Small Ones," said Wortsley. "Small Prayers are just as important as Big Ones to the person who is doing the praying."

"Small Urgent Prayers, to begin with!" said Fred, happily.

* * *

The next morning Wortsley took Fred to the stores and allowed him to pick his Cloud for dashing about on, a pair of Wings to practise with for his Wings Test, a case to carry them in when they weren't in use, and a map of the part of Glasgow where he was to look after Small Urgent Prayers.

"Great!" said Fred, and off he went.

His first job was an Urgent Prayer about Sarah's lost kitten.

Zoom!

Off went Fred on his Cloud until he spied the kitten, which was wandering up the Bearsden Road.

Fred couldn't just zoom down and grab it. That isn't the way Angels do things. He had to rush back to Sarah and make her think it would be a good idea to ask her dad to look for the kitten. *Then* he had to make her dad agree to go out and search, even though he was tired after a hard day at the hospital, and *then* Fred had to make Sarah's dad turn left, not right, at the crossroads, *and* he had to make sure Sarah's kitten wasn't run over by a lorry.

"Wasn't that lucky, Sarah?" Sarah's dad said when he came home with the kitten.

"Yes, it was!" said Sarah, who had forgotten all about her Small Urgent Prayer in the excitement, but

Fred didn't mind. He was only doing his job.

The next Prayer was easy, because Gran wanted Baby Alicia to go to sleep. Normally Fred would have sung to Alicia but Wortsley had said he wasn't allowed to sing, so Fred played his harp instead. Angels' harps are *odd*, and Fred's playing interfered with TV reception. A lot of people got cross and shouted rude things, but Fred, being an Angel, didn't understand the rude things, and he went on playing until Baby Alicia went to sleep.

The next Prayer looked easy, but it wasn't. It was from a farmer who wanted rain to make things grow. When Fred went to check the records he found that there was already a Prayer on file from Darren, the Angel who had had the job before him. Little Tom Cosgrave wanted fine weather for his picnic with Catherine and James.

Fred didn't know what to do, so he asked Wortsley.

"When is the picnic?" asked Wortsley.

"Three until five," said Fred.

"Let it rain up to two o'clock, then have sunshine until six, and then it can rain again for the farmer," said Wortsley, and that is what Fred arranged. Angels are very fair about Prayers, and try to get them right, when they can.

The farmer got his rain, and little Tom Cosgrave got sun for his picnic with Catherine and James.

Then Fred got a Prayer for a new doll, which he turned down because the girl had ten already. After that, he got one to stop toothache hurting, which was silly, because the tooth only hurt because it needed filling. If it wasn't filled, it would hurt much more in the end. Next he got half a dozen prayers, one after the other, for Our-Team-to-Score-a-Goal, and he granted them all because they came three-a-side, and that made the result of the football match a draw, three goals each.

By this time Fred was tired out, so he thought he would zoom back to Heaven for some refreshment. He parked his Cloud outside the Golden Gates and went in for some Wine and Honey and a smile from Hermione, the Loveliest Angel of Them All. When he came out again, his Cloud was *gone*!

"Gone!" gasped Fred, in dismay.

"What's gone?" said Wortsley, who as Chief Inspector of Angels had been fluttering close to Fred most of the morning, although Fred hadn't seen him.

"My Cloud," said Fred. "I left it outside, and now somebody has gone off on it."

"I see," said Wortsley.

"It was a nice one too," said Fred. "I picked that one specially when you showed it to me, because it was pink. There aren't many pink Clouds around."

"I know," said Wortsley.

He knew, because Wortsley had *made* Fred take that particular Cloud, in the same way that Fred *made* Sarah's dad go out to look for the kitten. That is the way that Angels do things.

"Now it is gone!" said Fred.

"What are you going to do about it?" asked Wortsley.

"Go and look for it, I suppose," said Fred, beginning to sound grumpy. Angels shouldn't be grumpy, and Fred knew that, but he was proud of his Cloud and very upset at losing it.

"If that is what you think best, you must do it," said Wortsley. "Borrow one of the old grey clouds from the store."

Fred took one of the grey clouds. It was tatty round the edges and not in the least pink. It wasn't very fast, but it was the best of a bad bunch. He went off on it to hunt for his Cloud.

He went round the Gorbals, and through Cardonnel, and over to Ibrox, and round Parkhead, but he couldn't find his Cloud anywhere.

Fred went back to Heaven for a quick hymn to cheer himself up, and then he met his friend Oscar, the Poetic Angel, and he asked Oscar if Oscar had seen a missing pink Cloud.

"Hmm," said Oscar. "Where did you get it?"

"Wortsley gave it to me," said Fred.

"Oh, *did* he!" said Oscar, and he zoomed off on his Cloud to give a poetry reading from his very own book of poems, without so much as trying to be helpful.

"Very badly behaved for an Angel, I must say!" grumbled Fred.

"Do you think so?" said Wortsley, popping up from just behind Fred yet again.

"Just like a Poet!" said Fred. "Head in the clouds! No time to be helpful."

"Maybe he was trying to help by *not* helping, Fred," said Wortsley.

"How can not helping be helpful?" asked Fred.

"Perhaps he knew it was important for you to think it out yourself," said Wortsley.

"I have thought about it," said Fred impatiently. "I have been dashing all over Glasgow thinking about it."

"Do you do your best thinking dashing about?" asked Wortsley, and Fred shook his head. "I suggest you try again. I'm afraid if you can't think it out for yourself, you're going to fail your First Test."

"Oh dear!" said Fred. "Oh dear, oh dear, oh dear!" And he rushed off to look for his Cloud again.

"Don't rush, Fred!" called Wortsley.

"Sorry," said Fred.

Fred went on very slowly. He had another look around Glasgow, checking out the airport and the railway station and Sauchiehall Street. It was past six o'clock by now and raining, just as Fred had arranged for the farmer, so there were plenty of clouds. But none of them were pink.

I'm going to fail my First Test, and then Wortsley won't let me be an Angel after all, Fred thought, miserably.

"I must cheer myself up," he said. Angels are supposed to be cheerful, not miserable, so Fred went off to Tom Cosgrave's house, and the farmer's house and Baby Alicia's house and the footballers' houses and Sarah's house to cheer himself up, but it didn't work.

"They're all so happy now! I wish it was as easy for me!" Fred muttered.

"Why is it easy for them?" asked Wortsley, putting in another of his surprise appearances by Fred's side. Fred was perched on the top branch of the tall tree in Sarah's garden, and Wortsley almost knocked him off it.

"When they had problems, all they had to do was pray, and an Angel popped down to help them!" said Fred.

"Ahem! Ahem!" said Wortsley, and he started whistling and looking at the sky.

"Pray?" asked Fred. "It wouldn't work, would it?"

"If you don't believe in Prayers, nobody will!" said Wortsley, rather impatiently.

"Just a little one, a quickie?" said Fred, doubtfully.

"Speed is not important," said Wortsley.

So Fred tried a Prayer … and the Prayer *worked*!

"One pink Cloud," said Wortsley as the Cloud came drifting down to the top of the tree in Sarah's garden.

"My Cloud!" said Fred.

"Rather good, that, I thought!" said Wortsley. "I may be Chief Inspector of Angels, but I can still do my bit when it comes to Small Urgent Prayers, if requested!"

"Wortsley," said Fred nervously. "Does … does this mean I've failed?"

"No!" said Wortsley. "You've passed! No one can be an Angel who doesn't believe in Prayer! You can continue as usual, Fred!"

"Oh, Wortsley!" said Fred delightedly. "Thank you very, very much!"

"Don't thank me," said Wortsley. "Just say a little Prayer!"

BEWARE OLGA!

by GILLIAN CROSS
illustrated by ARTHUR ROBINS

Fiona hated crusts. And skin and peel and all the tough, chewy outsides of things. But people never stopped nagging her about them.

"Eat your apple peel," said her mother. "It'll give you rosy cheeks."

Fiona cut off the peel and hung it on the washing-line for the birds.

"Don't leave your potato jackets!" her father said. "They'll make your eyes sparkle."

Fiona screwed them up and shot them through the window with her catapult.

"Finish your crusts," said her grandmother. "They'll give you nice curly hair."

"Who wants curly hair?"

Fiona hid the crusts in her pocket and took them down the garden to feed the hedgehog.

No one could make her eat the outside of

anything. Until the day she went down to the baker's to buy the bread on her own.

It was nearly closing time. She roller-skated all the way down the hill and straight into the shop.

"A large brown loaf and three doughnuts, please," Fiona said.

"Yes, *ma'am!*" The baker put them into her backpack and smiled at her.

"How about a little treat? A nice crusty roll?" he said.

"No, thank you! I don't like crusts," Fiona replied.

"You don't like – well, bless my soul!"

The baker leaned over the counter to look at her more closely.

"Everyone knows the crust's the best part," the baker said. "It makes your hair curl."

"I don't want curly hair," said Fiona. "Crusts are horrible. So is rice pudding skin. And apple peel. And everything that comes on the outside of food. I hate outsides."

"Do you now?" said the baker. "Well, fancy that. Maybe I ought to send my friend Olga to see you. She *loves* outsides." And he stood in the shop doorway, watching Fiona thoughtfully as she skated back up the hill.

The next day, just before tea, Fiona was in the garden, making a dam. She saw a reflection in the pond and looked up.

There stood a strange girl, exactly as tall as Fiona, but quite different. Her teeth gleamed, her cheeks were rosy and her hair stuck out in corkscrew curls.

"Hello," said the girl, "I'm Olga. The baker sent me. Can I come to tea?"

Fiona blinked. "Well – er –"

Before Fiona could get any further, Olga was at the back door, waiting to be let in.

Fiona opened the door and called, "Mum!"

Her mother yelled back, from upstairs. "I'm busy. Your tea's on the table."

"Tea!" said Olga.

ZAP! She was through the door and into the dining-room. When Fiona caught up with her, she was gazing at the table.

She snatched up a cheese sandwich and – ZAP! –

all the crust was gone. Grinning, she flicked the sandwich across the table on to Fiona's plate and picked up another one.

Fiona started to eat the sandwich, but she was only halfway through when Olga tossed her the second one. And then another and another. In ten minutes there was nothing left. Not even a crust.

"What's next?" Olga said.

Fiona swallowed her last mouthful and looked at the table.

"Warm milk and blancmange," she said. "And then little cakes."

Olga looked at the warm milk and her eyes gleamed. "Skin!"

She grabbed the mug and hooked the skin off with her long, pink tongue. Then she passed the milk back to Fiona.

"Fantastic!" Fiona took the milk and looked hopefully at the blancmange. "Could you…?"

Olga smiled.

ZAP!

The blancmange skin vanished.

Fiona grinned. "This is really good!" and she took a huge spoonful of blancmange.

Before she could swallow it, Olga turned to the cakes. "Outsides for me, insides for you. OK?"

Fiona's mouth was full of blancmange. She wanted to stop Olga, but she couldn't get the words out quickly enough.

ZAP! Before Fiona could speak, Olga ate all the icing and left the plain cakes.

"That's not fair," Fiona said.

Olga tossed her curls. "Yes, it is. You don't like outsides."

"I like *icing.*"

"Icing is *outside.* Icing makes your fingernails shine. What's next?"

Olga looked round and saw the fruit bowl on the sideboard.

ZAP! Before Fiona could stop her, she had eaten all the apple peel. And the banana skins.

Fiona stared at the bananas for a moment, feeling rather peculiar. Then she grabbed the fruit bowl and pushed it into the sideboard, to save the grapes. When she turned round, the room was empty, and there were strange slurping noises coming from the kitchen.

Slurp! Slurp! Olga was sitting on the floor by the fridge, licking cream off the trifle and eating the outside of the sausage rolls.

"Stop!" Fiona grabbed Olga's shoulder and tried to drag her away, but it was impossible. She was as solid as a rock. Olga grinned and grabbed three yogurt cartons out of the fridge.

"That's silly," said Fiona. "Yogurt hasn't got an outside."

"Oh, yes it has!" cried Olga.

"But…"

"Delicious outsides."

Olga bit into the plastic carton, chewing it up like a biscuit. The yogurt dribbled down her chin and ran all over the floor.

Olga licked her lips.

And reached for a milk bottle.

89

Fiona ran into the hall and grabbed her skateboard. There was only one thing to do. A second later she was whizzing down the hill towards the baker's shop.

She zoomed in at the door, bumped into an old lady buying a cream cake, and went sailing up in the air.

She landed behind the counter and the baker looked down at her.

"Olga?"

"Yes!" wailed Fiona. "How do I get rid of her?"

"Hmm. We'll have to see about that." The baker pulled the end off a loaf and began to chew it. Then he pulled off another bit and held it out to Fiona.

"But I don't…" she started to say.

He looked at her.

She took the crust and bit into it and the baker smiled.

"There's only one way to get rid of Olga," the baker said.

"Please tell me!"

"You've got to get her to eat the inside of something."

"But she won't!"

The baker smiled again. He reached under the counter and pulled out a piece of paper. "Try this."

Pineapple upside-down cake, it said. Chewing her crust, Fiona trudged back up the hill, reading the piece of paper as she went.

She pushed open the kitchen door and…

Wheee-bam!

She slipped on a raw egg white, skidded across the floor and landed in a puddle of baked beans.

Olga was eating the tins!

There were big bites out of the jamjars too. And the cornflakes packet. And the orange squash bottles. And the sugar bags. The things from *inside* were scattered everywhere.

And Olga was grinning. "Lovely outsides!"

Fiona forced herself to grin back. But she didn't waste any time. She grabbed a bowl and started to scoop things up – flour and butter and sugar. Eggs and milk and golden syrup.

And pineapple rings.

Olga watched suspiciously. "What are you doing?"

"Making a *delicious* pudding," said Fiona.

Olga licked her lips. "Insides for you, outsides for me?"

"All right." Fiona smiled cunningly. "Could you fetch some spoons? They're in the sideboard. Next to the grapes."

"Grapes!" Olga's eyes gleamed and she was off – ZAP!

Quick as a flash, Fiona poured the golden syrup into a glass dish and dropped in the pineapple rings, spooned the cake mixture on top and pushed the dish into the microwave.

Then she peeped into the dining-room. Olga was busy eating grape skins.

Fiona smiled.

The moment the upside-down cake was cooked, she took it out of the microwave. The sponge outside was set, and through the glass she could see the inside – delicious, sticky pineapple.

Running a knife round the edge of the sponge, she put a plate over the dish and turned the whole thing over.

The sponge fell on to the plate with the pineapple on top and the sticky pineapple juice running down the sides.

The sponge outside was inside and the pineapple inside was outside.

Fiona looked towards the dining-room door.

ZAP! There was Olga, at the table, with a spoon in her hand.

As Fiona put the pudding on the table, Olga stared at it, licking her lips with her long, pink tongue. Then the pineapple vanished and only the plain sponge was left. Olga pushed the pudding across to Fiona.

"You can have that," said Olga.

Fiona took a deep breath. "I don't like outsides," she said.

"Outsides?" Olga looked down at the remains of the pudding and turned pale. *"What was that?"*

"Pineapple upside-down cake."

Olga stared for a moment and then she shrieked. *"Aaaarrgh!"*

Her hair shot out all over her head in long, straight spikes. Her rosy cheeks turned green and her neat, white teeth cracked from top to bottom. She jumped to her feet and pointed her finger at Fiona. "You!"

Quick as a flash, Fiona snatched up a sausage roll with all the outside gone.

"Here you are!" she shouted. "More nice insides!"

Olga gave a loud, terrible wail and towered up, taller and taller and thinner and thinner until – ZAP! – there was a flash of light and a puff of thick, black smoke. Olga vanished – and a whirlwind hit the kitchen.

Tins appeared from nowhere and baked beans jumped back into them. Milk slurped into bottles and

cornflakes rattled into packets. Eggshells flew through the air and snapped together, and cream squirted itself, in swirls, on to the trifle.

In ten seconds, the kitchen was back to normal. Fiona looked round and grinned. Then she got up and walked into the dining-room.

The fruit bowl was standing on the sideboard. The apples had their peel back, and so did the bananas. And each grape had its own, unbroken skin.

Thank goodness! thought Fiona. Everything's come back! Then she remembered something and she turned round to look at the table.

All the crusts from her sandwiches had come back too. There they were, piled up in a big heap.

For a moment she stared at them, thinking about Olga. Then she sat down. Quickly she chewed each crust and swallowed it, until there were none left.

Just in case.

From that day on Fiona ate every crust she was given. Blancmange skin, too. *And* apple peel. *And* every other skin and rind and peel. She wasn't taking any risks.

Her cheeks grew rosy and her eyes sparkled, her teeth gleamed and her fingernails shone. And her hair was beautifully …

(Even grown-ups don't know everything.)

HOLLY
AND THE
SKYBOARD

by IAN WHYBROW
illustrated by TONY KENYON

On the morning of Holly's seventh birthday, Holly got up and did her chores as usual, even though it was her special day.

When she felt she'd done a good job, she opened her present from her mum and dad. It was a hand-knitted pullover with a skateboard pattern on the front.

Holly said it would look good with her red hair.

"Sorry we couldn't afford a real skateboard," sighed Dad. He knew how much Holly had wanted one.

Her mum said, "There's a lovely surprise for you today. Guess what! Your cousin Richard is coming over to play with you! Won't that be nice?"

Holly didn't like telling lies, but her mum looked so pleased, she couldn't hurt her feelings. "Just what I wanted on my birthday!" she said bravely.

Richard arrived in a big car driven by his nanny. He was a big rude boy with a big bottom. He was carrying the most *unbelievably* expensive skateboard in the whole world, all covered in fabulous stickers.

He also had a very small package which he gave to Holly.

"Here you are, Carrot Head," he said. "It's a book of stamps. Don't forget to stick one on your thank you letter, will you? Good joke, eh?" And he laughed, blah ha ha!

I wish he wouldn't call me Carrot Head, thought Holly.

Five minutes after Richard arrived, he said, "This is so *boring*! What are we supposed to do all day when you haven't even got a telly in this dump?"

"Why don't we go skateboarding?" Holly suggested. Every night, ever since she could remember, Holly had dreamed about skateboards. In the dream she had a skateboard with magic buttons on it. If she wanted to do a fantastic trick, all she had to do was press a button.

She looked longingly at Richard's skateboard, hoping that perhaps he would let her try it out.

"No way!" Richard snapped. "I bet you haven't even got a skatepark here or anything."

Holly said no, they didn't have a skatepark, but there was a quiet bit of roadway out the back. "Why don't we go and see?" she said.

There was a good slope that went down and down, then up in front of some big blue garage doors.

"There are some super bumpy parts here," said Holly. "They would be fun for lying down. And there's a drain to dodge by the kerb."

"What do you know about it, *girly*?" said Richard. "And what does that stupid old man want?"

Holly turned to see her next-door neighbour, Mr Windrush, waving to her over his back gate.

"Happy birthday, Holly," he called. "Would you and your cousin like to come into the workshop and see the present I've made for you?"

"*I'm* not coming!" shouted Richard. "I hate home-made presents!" And with that, he jumped on his fancy skateboard and whizzed off down the slope.

Holly ran over to the gate. "Don't take any notice of him, Mr Windrush," she said. "He's just a bit spoilt. He can't help being rude."

"Well," said the old man, "I hope you won't be disappointed. My work looks very rough and plain."

When Holly saw the skateboard lying on Mr Windrush's workbench, she wasn't just surprised; she was *astonished*. She jumped, just as if somebody had popped out from behind the sofa and shouted Hey! Because the skateboard was *exactly* like the one she had been riding in her dreams,

right down to the round buttons on the top! All she could say was, "Gosh, Mr Windrush! I don't *believe* it! Thank you, thank you, thank you!"

It made Mr Windrush very happy to see how pleased Holly was. He shut the gate after her, gave it a contented little pat and went indoors.

Richard was busy showing off, so he didn't notice that where the tips of Mr Windrush's fingers had tapped the gate, two little branches had sprung up and sprouted rainbow-coloured leaves and clusters of chocolate fudge bars.

"What a piece of *junk*!" laughed Richard, when he saw Holly's new skateboard.

Holly took no notice. She lay on her skateboard and enjoyed the lovely curvy feeling she got as it picked up speed down the slope.

"Too peasy!" shouted Richard. "Watch me and I'll show you what you can do on a *real* skateboard!"

He turned his hat round and showed Holly how he did Standies, Kneelies, Wheelies and Jumpies. He went really fast and he never fell off, not once.

Then he showed her the big lump of plastic at the back, so you could stamp down and make the board jump up. "Bet you haven't got *this*," he said.

"I haven't got any plastic, but I have got these special buttons," said Holly. She got off her board and pointed to the four round steel buttons set into the wood.

Richard laughed and said they were just screwheads. "They hold the wheels to the board, Carrot Cake!" he scoffed. "*Anybody's* got those. They're not special. Look!" He pressed down hard on one of his and showed her the white cross-shaped dent the screwhead made in his fingertip.

Holly had been thinking. Her birthday skateboard looked exactly the same as her dream skateboard – but perhaps it wouldn't *do* the same things in real life. Still, she held her breath, thought of her very favourite drink – and firmly pressed the top button on the left.

Suddenly Holly was sipping something delicious through a pink bendy straw – a cold Coca-Cola with a bubble gum ice-cream float and a cherry on top.

"Would *you* like one of these?" she asked.

Richard was so surprised, he fell flat on his big bottom. "Gimme one!" he shouted.

"Please," said Holly.

Richard had to say the word, even though he hated it.

"Please," he begged.

Holly pressed the button again and quick as a flash, Richard had a paper cup full of the most wonderful drink he had ever tasted – cold and fizzy, with a really big scoop of the best bubble gum ice-cream ever. *Ever!*

He couldn't believe his eyes. "Where did this come from?" he demanded.

"I just pressed one of the special buttons, that's all," explained Holly. She sucked hard and made the

Coke rattle in the bottom of her cup. "Ahhhh!" she gasped as she finished. "Just what I needed."

She put the empty paper cup down on her skateboard, and as soon as it touched the dull brown wood, the cup went *fffft* and vanished.

Richard's mouth dropped open in amazement.

"Let's go skateboarding!" laughed Holly.

For a minute, when Holly seemed to be doing magic tricks, Richard was lost for words. But as soon as he heard her say, "Let's go skateboarding!" he found his voice again.

"Watch me!" he yelled, dropping his cup. "Because this is going to be *hard*, Miss Special Buttons!"

He raced down the slope, screaming his head off, jigged to avoid a pothole, bent his knees and neatly bounced the skateboard up over a kerb, before spinning it round and stopping it in a flurry of dust in front of the garages.

"Try *that* on your stupid piece of wood," he panted.

Holly lay face down, her legs sticking out like a frog's.

That made Richard laugh. She took no notice, but

pointed herself down the slope, right at Richard, and kicked off with her toes.

With her nose just above the road, she was soon going even faster than Richard had done. As Holly rushed nearer, her red hair flying out behind her, Richard started to get nervous.

If she didn't do something soon – drag her baseball boots along the ground or roll off sideways – she would crash into the kerb, or be smashed to pieces against one of the garage doors!

Richard put his arm over his head and made himself as small as he could, expecting to be bowled over like a skittle. That was when Holly pressed a button and her skateboard lifted its nose and took off like a plane. It rose smoothly over the roofs of the garages, and then soared higher to skim the tops of some trees.

Holly looked down at the cottages below, shrunk to the size of toys. Richard looked no bigger than an earwig. Holly pulled up the nose of the skateboard and looped the loop. Then she leaned, swooping down to snatch a black and white feather from an empty magpie's nest, and stuck it in her hair. Pink smoke came out of the back of the skateboard and she wrote her name in joined-up letters in the sky. Then she dived and landed expertly on the road before rolling down to where Richard was still glued to the spot.

"Let's go in and have some lunch now, shall we?" Holly said, cool as a Coca-Cola with a bubble gum ice-cream float.

All through lunch Richard sat looking at the magpie feather in Holly's hair and wondering how he could get the magic skateboard off her. Finally, he had a very cunning idea.

When the car came for him, Richard ran up to Holly's mum and gave her a big kiss (which he had never done before) and said, "Thank you very much for having me," (which he had never done before) and then he said, "Before I go, I would like to give Holly my fabulous, expensive skateboard and I'll just have her ugly old home-made one. How about that?"

Holly was too surprised to answer, and as for her mum and dad, they thanked Richard for coming, thinking what a lucky girl Holly was to have such a generous cousin.

Holly wandered out into the garden with Richard's skateboard and sighed a sad sigh.

"What's the matter, Holly?" came a voice from the other side of the fence. "Has your cousin left you?"

"I hope you won't be upset, Mr Windrush," sniffed Holly, "but Richard's taken the lovely skateboard you made for me and left me his."

"I'm not at all upset, Holly," said Mr Windrush. "As a matter of fact, I'd say you made a jolly good swap. May I have a closer look?"

Holly passed it over the fence. Mr Windrush held it just with the tips of his fingers, touching the beautifully smooth wood and feeling the cool metal strip along its edge. "Why, this is a *dream* of a skateboard," he smiled, as he handed it back.

When she took it in her arms once more, Holly

was surprised to notice that it had four round steel buttons where the screwheads had been!

"Happy skyboarding, Holly!" said Mr Windrush.

Meanwhile, out on the motorway, there was a big traffic jam.

And in the middle of the big traffic jam there was a big car.

And in the back seat of the big car there was a big rude boy with a big bottom.

And the big boy with the big bottom let out a big scream.

Because no matter how hard he pressed the buttons on his home-made skateboard, all he got was a little white cross-shaped dent on the tip of his finger!

THE SNOW MAZE

by JAN MARK
illustrated by JAN ORMEROD

On the way to school Joe found a key. It was in the long grass, so he did not see it. He kicked it with his toe.

It flew into the air and clinked upon a stone. Then he saw it.

Joe picked up the key. He held it in the air and turned it round. It was not like the key of Joe's front door. It was like the key of the back door, but it was twice as long and three times heavier.

"Maybe a giant dropped this key," Joe said.

He took the key to school and showed it to Irrum.

"Maybe a giant dropped it," said Joe.

"Can I hold it?" Irrum said.

Joe let Irrum hold the key while he counted. It was a special way of counting. "One-elephant, two-elephant, three-elephant, four-elephant, five-elephant."

That was five whole seconds. Then he took it back. Other people came to look. Joe let each one hold it for five seconds, while he counted elephants. They thought it was a good key.

Then Akash came along. Joe tried to hide the key, but Akash saw it.

Akash laughed. He always laughed at Joe.

"That key is no good," Akash said. "Keys are no good unless they open something."

Then everyone laughed at Joe, except Irrum.

Everyone did what Akash did, except Irrum.

When everyone had gone away, Irrum said, "I think it is a good key. Perhaps it is magic. Perhaps it will open the lonely gate."

Joe passed the lonely gate when he went home from school.

It stood on its own between two gateposts.

On the other side of the gate was a grassy field, but Joe could get on to the field without going through the gate. There was no wall to keep him out. The wall had fallen down and the gate stood all alone. That was why it was called the lonely gate. No one ever went through it. It was locked.

The gate was made of wood. Ivy climbed up it.

Joe moved the ivy leaves and underneath there was a keyhole. He put his key in the lock and turned it. The key clicked. The lock squeaked. Joe pushed.

The ivy tried to hold shut the gate, but Joe pushed harder.

The ivy let go. The hinges screeched. The gate opened.

On the other side of the gate was the grassy field, with a path in it.

Joe looked at the path. It went round and round, backwards and forwards, in the grassy field. He had never seen it before.

Joe looked round the gatepost at the grassy field. There was no path.

The path was there only if he went through the gate. Perhaps Irrum was right, and he had found a magic key.

Joe began to walk along the path. He walked ten steps and then the path turned. Joe turned too.

Now he was walking back to the gate, but before he got there the path turned again. This time it went round the grassy field, but before it got back to the gate it turned again, and Joe turned too.

Joe and the path went backwards and forwards, round and round, and when the path stopped at last, Joe was right in the middle of the field.

He knew it was time to go home or his mum would worry, so he ran back, along the path, round and round, backwards and forwards, until he came to the gate.

He went out of the gate and locked it. He looked round the gatepost. There was no path.

Irrum was right. He had found a magic key.

* * *

When Joe went to school next day he passed the lonely gate. He looked at the grassy field. There was no path. He opened the gate with his key.

The path was there.

He locked the gate again.

At school, he said to Miss, "What do you call it when a path goes round and round, backwards and forwards, all folded up?"

"I think that's a maze," said Miss.

"No it's not," Tim said. "I went in a maze with my mum. It had high hedges. We got lost."

"Not all mazes have hedges," Miss said. "Some are made of turf. Turf is grass."

"How can you get lost in grass?" Tim said.

"You don't get lost in a turf maze," Miss said. "It's a magic pattern. You run along the path."

"Boring," said Akash. He did not believe in magic.

"How did you know about the maze, Joe?" Miss asked.

Joe did not want to tell. "I saw a picture," he said.

"Once there was a turf maze near this school," Miss told them. "But it was lost, long ago."

"That was careless," Akash said.

"How can you lose a maze?" Tim asked.

"Perhaps a farmer ploughed over it," Irrum said.

"I know where that maze is," Joe said to himself.

After school he went to the lonely gate and opened it with his key. Then he saw Akash, down by the pillar box, so he closed the gate and locked it behind him. He ran round the path to the middle of the maze.

Akash stood in the road and shouted.

"Why are you going round and round like that?"

"I'm running my maze," Joe said.

"I can't see any maze," Akash said. "I think you're mad."

Joe stepped out of the maze and went over to stand by Akash. He looked back. The maze was not there.

"It's a secret maze," Joe said. "I'm the only one who can see it."

"Huh! You are mad," Akash said.

Akash was big and strong. He was not a bully, but people did what he told them to.

Tim was not a bully either, but he wanted to be like Akash.

When Akash said something, Tim said it too.

Next day, at school, Akash said, "Joe's mad. He can see things that are not there."

"Joe's mad," said Tim. "Joe's bad." He did not think Joe was bad, but he liked the sound of it.

"Mad Joe, bad Joe, sad Joe," the others shouted.

"Joe's got a maze," Akash said. "Mazy Joe!"

"Joe's mazy," said Tim. "Joe's crazy."

"Mazy, crazy, lazy Joe," the others shouted. They all ran round and round in the playground, pretending to be Joe.

"This is what Joe does," Akash said, and the others followed him.

Irrum did not run or shout.

"Stupid people," Irrum said, and stood still, while the others ran about.

She stood on the edge of the playground, but Joe was in the middle. The others ran rings round him. People pushed him as they went past.

"Crazy Joe!" Akash shouted.

Joe did not want to be like Akash, big and strong. He wanted to be like Irrum, small and brave.

At home time Joe ran from school and opened the lonely gate. Then he ran his secret maze.

Akash told the others where he went. They followed Joe, but Joe had his key, and they could not go through the gate into the maze. They stood in the road and laughed at Joe, running round and round, backwards and forwards. They could not see the maze.

Tim said that Joe was making it up.

Sometimes they all came and ran about on the grassy field, but only Joe could see the maze, because he had gone through the gate. It was his secret.

Next day when Joe came to school, Akash and Tim shouted, "Mad, sad, bad Joe!"

"Mazy, crazy, lazy Joe!" the others shouted, and ran rings round Joe in the middle of the playground.

Irrum stood beside him.

"Crazy, lazy, mazy," Akash yelled.

"Stupid people," Irrum said.

Miss came out to see what they were doing.

"We're playing mazes, Miss," said Tim.

Miss laughed. "That's good," she said. She could not hear what they were shouting.

At break Joe stayed indoors and helped Miss find

lost scissors. At lunchtime he hid in the toilets. At afternoon play it rained and they could not go out. Miss sent them to the hall to run about. The maze game started again. Joe sat under a table and held his key.

Irrum went up to Akash.

Akash was yelling. "Mad, sad. Crazy, mazy!"

"I'd rather be crazy than nasty," Irrum said. "I'd rather be sad than stupid."

"You don't want to be like mazy Joe," Tim said.

"I don't want to be like you," said Irrum, and she did not run away.

When people were rude to Tim and Akash, they ran away quickly. Irrum just stood, and stared and glared. Tim and Akash went on shouting, but they did not shout so loudly.

Joe wished he were small and brave, like Irrum, but he was only small.

After school, he went away alone, and opened the gate with his key. He ran his maze, all alone.

One morning Joe saw Irrum standing by the lonely gate.

Irrum said, "Show me your maze, Joe."

"No," said Joe.

"But I believe you," Irrum said. "I don't think you're making it up."

Then Joe remembered how Irrum had told him that the key might open the lonely gate. He remembered how Irrum stood beside him when the others played mazes.

"All right," said Joe, and he unlocked the gate.

"Can you see the maze?" Joe said.

"Yes," said Irrum.

"Run round it then," Joe said, in case she was pretending, and Irrum ran along the path. She could see it too.

Joe looked round the gatepost at the grassy field. All he could see was Irrum, running, backwards and forwards, round and round. The maze was invisible.

Every day after that, Joe and Irrum unlocked the lonely gate, when no one was looking. They ran the maze.

The others came and stood in the road and laughed. They could see Irrum and Joe, but the maze was invisible.

One morning it was cold and there was white frost on the grassy field. When Irrum and Joe unlocked the gate and ran the maze, they left footprints.

No one else was there.

Afterwards Joe locked the gate and they looked round the gatepost. The maze was invisible, but the footprints were still there, running round and round, backwards and forwards.

"Let's show the others," Irrum said.

"No," said Joe.

"But now they will believe you," Irrum said.

Joe thought about this all day.

He wanted to be believed, but he wanted to keep his secret maze.

At home time some snowflakes fell. Joe and Irrum ran to the grassy field and the footprints were still there, in the frost. They had not melted, but the snow was beginning to cover them up.

Joe unlocked the gate and they started to run the maze, round and round, backwards and forwards.

The snow got deeper and deeper, so they ran the maze again, to keep the path open.

The others came along. They stood in the road and watched. Then they ran on to the grassy field.

"Stop them," Irrum said. "Their footprints will spoil our footprints and we will lose the maze."

Joe stood still. He thought.

"Go back!" he shouted. "I'll let you in through the lonely gate."

The others went back. Joe unlocked the gate and let them in.

"Can you see the maze?" Irrum said, and they all said, "Yes".

"Then follow me," said Joe, and they all ran the maze, one behind the other. When they got to the middle they turned round and went back to the gate. But the snow was still falling, so they turned round and ran the maze again.

And then Irrum said, "Look!"

There in the road was her mum, and Joe's mum, and Akash's granny and Tim's dad. Miss was there too. They had come to look for the children, all the mums and dads and grannies.

They stood in a row and looked at the grassy field. Now it was a field of snow.

"What can you see?" called Joe, and they all called back, "We can see a maze!"

It was not a turf maze any longer. It was a snow maze. Everyone could see it now.

The snow fell faster and thicker.

"What shall we do?" said Miss. "The children have found the lost maze. We must not lose it again."

Tim's dad was a builder. He ran through the snow to fetch sand in a barrow.

Then he followed the footprints, backwards and forwards, round and round the maze, and poured sand into them.

Right away the snow covered the sand.

"But when it melts," said Irrum's mum, "the sand will still be there."

"And the maze will still be there," Akash said.

He laughed. He was not laughing at Joe, he was laughing because he was pleased about the maze, so Joe laughed too.

Akash was right. When the snow melted, the sand maze was still there on the grassy field. People came with spades and cut out the path, and so the maze was there for always, and everyone could see it.

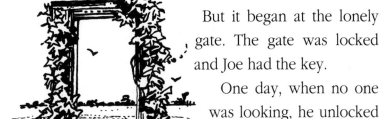

But it began at the lonely gate. The gate was locked and Joe had the key.

One day, when no one was looking, he unlocked the lonely gate for the last time. He left it standing open, so anyone could run the maze whenever they wanted to. It was not a secret maze any more, and the gate was no longer lonely.

Everyone was pleased because the children had found the lost maze.

"Joe found it," Irrum said.

"How did you find it, Joe?" asked Miss.

"Irrum told me where to look," said Joe.

"How did Irrum know where to look?" asked Miss.

"I just told him to open the lonely gate," Irrum said. She did not tell about the key.

After school Joe took the key and went back to the place where he had found it. He hid the key in the long grass.

One day the maze might be lost again.

One day, someone else might find the key.

THE MAGIC BOATHOUSE

by SAM LLEWELLYN
illustrated by ARTHUR ROBINS

The minibus of the School for Forgotten Orphans was rambling down a winding lane in the bottom of a deep valley, crammed with forgotten orphans heading for their holiday.

Joe and his sister Doris were at the back, as usual. The Fat Ern mob were at the front, hitting each other. The Soppy Emmer mob were behind them, gooing at their dollies.

The reason Joe and Doris were at the back was that Joe did not like hitting people unless he had to, so Fat Ern's mob said he was soppy. And Doris did not like playing with dolls, or anyway not all the time, so Soppy Emmer's mob said she was fat.

There was plenty of noise in the minibus.

"Shurrup!" roared horrible Mr Barge. He was the driver, and the teacher in charge of the holiday.

The Fat Ern mob shurruped. The Soppy Emmer mob shurruped.

Joe and Doris were so excited they did not even hear.

"You will be punished!" bellowed Mr Barge, who hated Joe and Doris because they were not evil enough and they did not fit in.

The minibus bounced on in silence. The road stopped. Grey waves were bursting on a rocky beach, their spray splattering an ancient cottage.

Fat Ern said, "There's no electric wires."

"Pafetic!" said the mob, real tough.

Soppy Emmer said, "It looks really *old*."

"Disgustin'!" cried the gang, real indignant.

Joe thought it all looked extremely interesting, but

kept his mouth shut in case the Fat Ern mob bashed him one.

Doris thought it all looked lovely, but kept her mouth shut in case the Soppy Emmer gang made her change the nappies on their dollies.

The air was full of the cry of gulls.

Fat Ern turned on his ghetto-blaster. Soppy Emmer began to sing along. The racket was huge.

"ORRIGHT," roared Mr Barge. "UNPACK!"

The cottage smelt of paraffin. There were three rooms upstairs.

"RIGHT," yelled Mr Barge. "GIRLS THIS SIDE. BOYS THAT SIDE! ME IN HERE!"

Fat Ern and his mob looked at Joe. "We're not sleepin' with *'im*," they said.

Soppy Emmer and her gang looked at Doris. "We're not sleepin' with *'er*," they said.

UP YOU GO!

"Quite right," yelled Mr Barge. There was a ladder leading to a trapdoor in the ceiling. "You two can sleep up there," he said.

Up there was a small room with a circular window and two rickety beds.

"I like it up here," said Doris.

"Me too," said Joe. "But don't tell them, or they'll change us."

"Right!" roared Mr Barge when they had all unrolled their sleeping bags and were downstairs in the cobwebby sitting-room. "Lovely nature walk next. Except Joe and Doris. Joe and Doris, clean up."

"Why?" said Joe.

"Because of not shutting up when *told* to!" yelled Mr Barge.

"That's unfair," said Doris.

"Cheek!" howled Mr Barge, blue in the face. "You're off tomorrow's outing, too. The rest follow me!"

And they filed over the horizon, Fat Ern's mob punching each other, Soppy Emmer's gang plaiting each other's hair.

"Clear up, ho," said Doris. But the cobwebs in the house were thick as knitting.

"Let's start in the garden," said Joe. But the rose bushes were like barbed wire entanglements.

"Let's go exploring," they both said at once.

So they walked on to the beach, where they found a boathouse.

"Must belong to the cottage," said Doris.

In they went.

There were cobwebs, a mouldy lobster pot and a lot of darkness. And hanging on the wall, a thing that looked like a giant ice-cream cone. Joe unhung it.

"It's made of brass," he said.

"Looks like a sort of hooter," said Doris.

"Wrong," said a voice. It was an old, slow voice. It nearly made Joe and Doris jump out of their skins. "It's a foghorn."

As their eyes got used to the gloom, Doris and Joe saw an old man.

Then a shadow darkened the doorway: a fat shadow, with no neck. It was Fat Ern.

"Bunked orf," said Fat Ern, snatching the foghorn out of Joe's hand and eyeing it scornfully. "Can't stand nature."

The old man said, "Blow that horn."

"Blow it yourself, Grandad," said Fat Ern, whose manners were diabolical.

"I'll do it," said Joe, whose manners were fine. He took the foghorn in his hand. It looked old. In fact it looked ancient. He walked outside, on to the beach, and blew.

The horn made a curious sound. Doris had the idea that it was fading not so much into the *distance* as into the *past*. As the last echoes died, sky and sea turned pearly grey, and the cliffs and the horizon disappeared.

"Foghorn," said the old man, cackling. "Brings the fog. And other things."

A noise came out of the fog – a creak and thump, creak and thump, as of many oars. The grey blanket thinned and cleared.

There was a ship in the bay. It had a mast and oars, and a huge eye painted at its front end.

130

It swept up to the beach. Men swarmed down a
gangplank.

The old man said, "They're the Roman Invasion!"

One of the Romans clanked up the beach and said

something in a foreign language, probably (thought Joe, who owned an excellent encyclopedia) Latin.

"He wants to know for what task you called 'im," said the old man. "But there's a catch – "

Joe thought. "Tidy up the garden, please," he said.

The small soldier clashed his spear across his breastplate.

Orders were shouted.

Someone started a bonfire. In the smoke Joe and Doris could not see exactly what was happening, but it looked like a lot.

* *The garden is divided into three parts.*
** *Cotta has fallen into the ditch!*
*** *Bring a ladder!*

In about twenty minutes, the small soldier was back.

"He says the task is finished," said the old man.

The small soldier smiled. Then his dark eyes lit on Fat Ern, and he began to jabber.

"He wants you for a gladiator," said the old man.

"Yay!" cried Ern. "Aw right!"

The Roman walked Fat Ern down the beach and up the gangplank. The fog came down again. There was the sound of the oars.

When the fog cleared, the ship was gone.

The cottage's weedy garden and snaky paths had gone too. Instead, a straight road of white stone led to the front door, beside which a golden oriole was singing in a bay tree.

"That was quick," said Joe.

"I don't call two thousand years partickler quick," said the old man. "Here's the rest of your lot. See you tomorrow."

Even Mr Barge had to admit that Joe and Doris had done a fair job on the garden. But he still would not let them go on the walk to Hot Sands the next day.

"Tidy up the house," he yelled. "You've only done half the job. By the way, where's Ern?"

"He'll be back in time," said Doris, cleverly.

Mr Barge nodded. Ern would not be missed. In fact his mob was looking a lot happier already. Thug Ed was making a daisy-chain, and Karl the Killer was teaching a kitten to purr.

"Off we go," roared Mr Barge.

Once the file had gone up the hill and over the horizon, Doris and Joe went to the boathouse.

"Nice to see yer," said the old man. "Tidy the 'ouse, is it?"

Doris nodded.

A shadow crossed the open doorway; a soppy shadow, with ten bows in its pigtails. Soppy Emmer.

"I came *back*," said Soppy Emmer. "My shoe got muddy. Look." On her satin ballet pump, there was indeed a speck of earth.

The old man pointed at the foghorn. He said, "Blow that 'orn."

"Horrid dirty thing!" said Soppy Emmer. "I might get a virus. Blow it yourself!"

"Let me," said Doris, who was not fussy. She took the horn in her hand. She walked outside, on to the stony beach, and blew.

The horn made its curious sound. Joe had the idea that it was fading not so much into the *distance* as into the *past*. As the last echoes died, sky and sea turned pearly grey, and the cliffs and the horizon disappeared.

"Here they come," said the old man, sniffing.

Doris sniffed too. A powerful smell of cooking was wafting in from the sea. The fog cleared.

There was a ship in the bay. It had a prow like a dragon's head. It shot up to the beach and lay with its sails flapping. People jumped out and began to wade ashore.

Joe said, "More armour!"

The old man said, "What d'you expect? It's the Norman Conquest. By the way, there's a tiny catch –"

One of the Norman women trotted up the beach. She stopped in front of Doris and said something in a foreign language, probably (thought Doris, who shared the excellent encyclopedia with Joe) French.

"She wants to know for what task you called 'er," said the old man.

Doris thought. "Tidy the house, please," she said.

The Normans streamed up the beach, down the white road and into the cottage. Clouds of dust began billowing from the windows.

Doris and Joe could not see what was happening,

* *Eek! A hundred spiders!*
** *Ugh! A mouse's nest!*

but it looked like a lot. In about twenty minutes, a Norman woman was back.

"Says the task is finished," said the old man.

The Norman woman giggled. Then she saw Emmer. *"Oo la la!"* she cried, and began to talk with great excitement.

"Reckons you'll be red 'ot at needlework," said the old man. "Wants you to 'elp with that Bayeux Tapestry."

"Oo!" cried Soppy Emmer. "Faaaabyouless!"

The Norman lady walked Soppy Emmer down the beach and boosted her on to the ship. The fog came down again.

When it cleared, the ship was gone.

The cobwebs and the dust had gone too. The cottage was scrubbed clean, and sweet herbs had been strewn on the flagstones. Two large saucepans were bubbling on the kitchen range, sending out delicious smells.

"That was quick," said Doris.

"I don't call nine hundred and thirty-seven years partickerly quick," said the old man, pocketing a bottle of wine someone had left on the table. "Here's the rest of your lot. See you tomorrow."

Mr Barge sat down and ate a vast supper. Afterwards, he announced that everyone should play close to the cottage the next day. Then he looked about him as if something was missing. "Where's Emmer?" he howled.

"She's feeling a bit, er, sew-sew," said Joe, cleverly.

Mr Barge nodded and gulped down another glass of wine. Emmer would not be missed. In fact, her gang were looking a lot happier already. Delicate Daphne was wading around in some mud by the river, and Fragile Fiona was arm wrestling Breakable Bella.

So next morning they all stayed around the cottage. In the old days, the air would have been thick with teases and insults. But with Ern and Emmer gone, everyone got on surprisingly well. They even talked to Joe and Doris.

But Mr Barge mooched around with his hands in

his pockets, sulking because he had no reason to shout at anybody.

Then he wandered off in the direction of the boathouse.

"Quick!" said Doris and Joe, both at once. "After him!"

They found Mr Barge standing in front of the old man. He was holding the foghorn.

"That there," the old man was saying, "is a foghorn."

"I know that!" barked Mr Barge.

"It summons fog," said the old man.

"Poppycock!" yelled Mr Barge, delighted to have found someone to shout at. "It is a warning device for seagoing craft in low visibility situations. Look," he bellowed, "one blows it thus." He raised the foghorn to his lips, and blew.

The foghorn blared. Joe and Doris had the feeling

that it was fading not so much into the *distance* as *underwater.* As the last echo died, sky and sea turned pearly grey and the cliffs and the horizon disappeared.

But this time, the echo did not *quite* die. It seemed to hang in the water, and in the rocks underfoot, and to become a huge and awful *bubbling*.

"Here it comes," said the old man, folding his deck-chair.

The fog was cold and full of a powerful smell of rotting fish fingers.

"By the way, there's a tiny catch – "

"What a ghastly smell!" yelled Mr Barge.

The old man was well up the beach now. Joe and Doris held hands. Out in the bay the sea was moiling sluggishly, as if a big paddle were stirring it from below.

"Obviously this is a pollution situation," Mr Barge was bellowing. "I shall complain…"

But nobody ever knew who Mr Barge thought he was going to complain to. Because a huge tentacle snaked out of the water like the lash of a whip, wrapped itself round his waist and flicked him into a vast mouth that had opened in the bay. There was a small, watery *crunch*.

And that was that.

"Waste of a perfectly good pair of khaki shorts," said the old man. "But there's no reasoning with that kraken." He stretched, and shoved the foghorn down his thigh boot.

"Thing you should remember," he said. "That tiny catch. When you blows the foghorn, them from the fog 'as to take one with 'em. I tried to say. Only they kept interruptin'."

The fog came down again.

When it cleared, the water in the bay was still. And the boathouse had gone, and the old man with it. And so had Mr Barge, and of course Fat Ern and Soppy Emmer.

So Joe and Doris walked back to the other kids and everyone cheered. Then they all had a great holiday which lasted for ever.

Acknowledgements

Tillie McGillie's Fantastical Chair
Text © 1992 Vivian French Illustrations © 1992 Sue Heap

'The Haunting" from *Crumbling Castle*
Text © 1989 Sarah Hayes Illustrations © 1989 Helen Craig

"Under the Moon" from *Under the Moon*
Text © 1993 Vivian French Illustrations © 1993 Chris Fisher

Beware the Killer Coat
Text © 1994 Susan Gates Illustrations © 1994 Josip Lizatović

"The Angel Who Lost His Cloud" from *Fred the Angel*
Text © 1989 Martin Waddell Illustrations © 1989 Patrick Benson

Beware Olga!
Text © 1993 Gillian Cross Illustrations © 1993 Arthur Robins

Holly and the Skyboard
Text © 1993 Ian Whybrow Illustrations © 1993 Tony Kenyon

The Snow Maze
Text © 1992 Jan Mark Illustrations © 1992 Jan Ormerod

The Magic Boathouse
Text © 1994 Sam Llewellyn Illustrations © 1994 Arthur Robins